CUSTOMS, CULTURE & CUISINE

*Love thy Neighbor.
Love thy Food.*

CHINESE

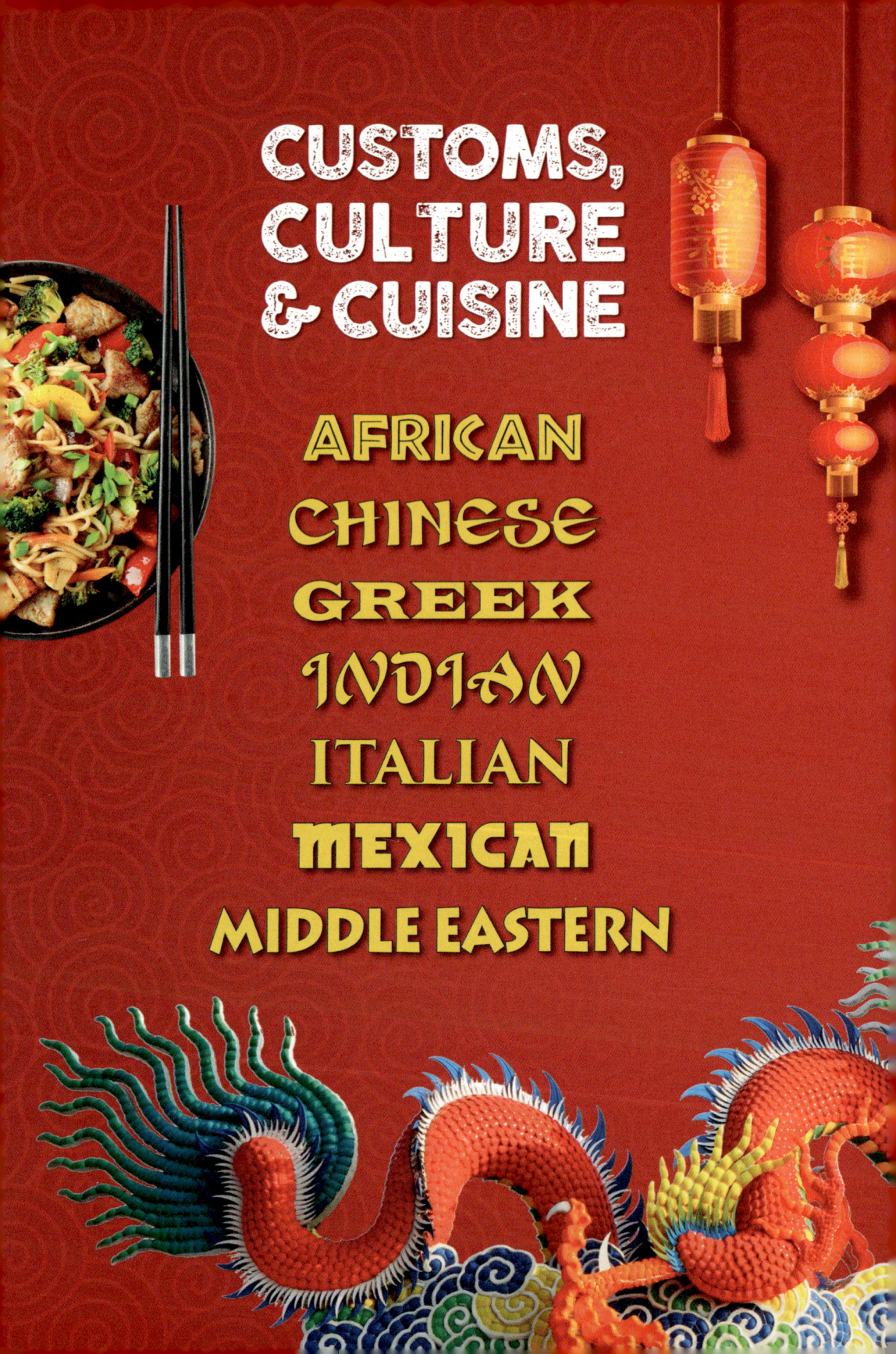

CUSTOMS, CULTURE & CUISINE

AFRICAN
CHINESE
GREEK
INDIAN
ITALIAN
MEXICAN
MIDDLE EASTERN

CUSTOMS, CULTURE & CUISINE

Peter Douglas

MC

MASON CREST
MIAMI

CHINESE

MASON CREST
PO Box 221876, Hollywood, FL 33022
(866) MCP-BOOK (toll-free) • www.masoncrest.com

Copyright © 2023 by Mason Crest, an imprint of National Highlights, Inc. All rights reserved. No part of this publication may be reproduced or transmitted in any form or by any means, electronic or mechanical, including photocopying, recording, taping, or any information storage and retrieval system, without permission in writing from the publisher.

Printed in the United States of America

First printing
9 8 7 6 5 4 3 2 1

ISBN (hardback) 978-1-4222-4677-1
ISBN (series) 978-1-4222-4675-7
ISBN (ebook) 978-1-4222-7136-0

Library of Congress Cataloging-in-Publication Data

Names: Douglas, Peter, 1968- author.
Title: Chinese / Peter Douglas.
Description: Hollywood, FL : Mason Crest, [2023] | Series: Customs, culture & cuisine | Includes bibliographical references and index.
Identifiers: LCCN 2022002787 | ISBN 9781422246771 (hardback) | ISBN 9781422246757 (series) | ISBN 9781422271360 (ebook)
Subjects: LCSH: Food habits—China—Juvenile literature. | Cooking, Chinese—Juvenile literature. | Cooking—China—Juvenile literature. | China—Social life and customs—Juvenile literature.
Classification: LCC GT2853.C6 D68 2023 | DDC 394.1/20952—dc23/eng/20220127
LC record available at https://lccn.loc.gov/2022002787

Developed and Produced by Crafted Content, LLC (www.craftedcontentllc.com)
Cover and Interior Design by Torque Advertising + Design

Publisher's Note: Websites listed in this book were active at the time of publication. The publisher is not responsible for websites that have changed their address or discontinued operation since the date of publication. The publisher reviews and updates the websites each time the book is reprinted.

QR CODES AND LINKS TO THIRD-PARTY CONTENT

You may gain access to certain third-party content ("Third-Party Sites") by scanning and using the QR Codes that appear in this publication (the "QR Codes"). We do not operate or control in any respect any information, products, or services on such Third-Party Sites linked to by us via the QR Codes included in this publication, and we assume no responsibility for any materials you may access using the QR Codes. Your use of the QR Codes may be subject to terms, limitations, or restrictions set forth in the applicable terms of use or otherwise established by the owners of the Third-Party Sites. Our linking to such Third-Party Sites via the QR Codes does not imply an endorsement or sponsorship of such Third-Party Sites or the information, products, or services offered on or through the Third-Party Sites, nor does it imply an endorsement or sponsorship of this publication by the owners of such Third-Party Sites.

CONTENTS

Introduction: 6
Chapter 1: Shandong 9
Chapter 2: Anhui & Fujian 21
Chapter 3: Sichuan & Hunan 37
Chapter 4: Zhejiang, Jiangsu & Guangdong 47
Chapter 5: Chinese Food in America 63
Research Project 74
Glossary of Key Terms 75
Further Reading 76
Internet Resources 77
Index 78
Author's Biography & Credits 80

KEY ICONS TO LOOK FOR:

Sidebars: This boxed material within the main text allows readers to build knowledge, gain insights, explore possibilities, and broaden their perspectives by weaving together additional information to provide realistic and holistic perspectives.

Educational Videos: Readers can view videos by scanning our QR codes, providing them with additional educational content to supplement the text. Examples include news coverage, moments in history, speeches, iconic sports moments, and much more!

Glossary of Key Terms: This back-of-the-book glossary contains terminology used throughout this book. Words found here increase the reader's ability to read and comprehend higher-level books and articles in this field.

Research Project: Readers are pointed toward an area of further inquiry that relates to each book and encourages deeper research and analysis.

INTRODUCTION

China is a vast country with diverse geography, history, and culture. As the fourth-largest country globally, it has about 1.4 billion people speaking different languages and dialects in more than 30 provinces, autonomous regions, and municipalities under its control. China's customs, cultures, and cuisine are as varied as the land itself.

This diversity is especially evident in the cuisine, with a wide variety of Chinese cuisine types found across the world's most populous nation. There are eight major cuisine types in China:

● **Shandong Cuisine:** This cuisine is from the northeast coast of China, where the seafood is the star, presented salty and always fresh.

● **Anhui and Fujian cuisines:** These mountainous regions in eastern China each feature cuisine that relies heavily on wild, local ingredients.

● **Sichuan and Hunan cuisines:** These two central inland regions are also known worldwide for their cuisine, which in both cases is famously spicy.

● **Zhejiang, Jiangsu, and Guangdong:** Guangdong is the home of Cantonese food, perhaps the best known of all Chinese cuisines internationally. All three regions offer excellent seafood dishes, but overall flavors are lighter and sweeter than in other regions.

One of the core principles behind Chinese cooking is balance in all things; this includes balancing sweet, salty, bitter, and sour flavors so that one flavor does not overpower the others. This principle can be used to create countless dishes with unique ingredients but similar styles or techniques.

Food is also used to bring balance and harmony in Chinese culture. Many customs and celebrations are centered around the shared experience of cooking and eating.

Chinese culture is often characterized as a balance between stability and change. The same can be said of the cuisine, which has been influenced by both Chinese food traditions and those from around Asia, Europe, and Africa over its millennia-long history. Food brings people together to share experiences with friends and family, and it helps to create memories that are cherished for years to come.

INGREDIENTS:

onions, garlic, vinegar, sea cucumber, pork, peanuts, millet, wheat, oats, barley, potatoes, tomatoes, cabbage, mushrooms, eggplant, corn, and ginger.

CHAPTER 1

Shandong

Shandong Province is situated on the northeast coast of China along the Yellow Sea. It is home to approximately 96 million people. The Yellow River has strongly influenced the culture of this region.

A River Runs Through It

The Yellow River basin covers about 280,000 square kilometers (174,000 square miles), an area almost as large as California or France. The river flows from west to east over a distance of more than 5,400 kilometers (3,355 miles) and serves as an important transportation route. It begins in Qinghai Province and flows into and through Shandong, ending at Laizhou Bay on the Bohai Sea, the largest gulf in the country.

Shandong has a long peninsula that extends eastward into the sea, separating the Bohai Sea in the north and the Yellow Sea to its south. It has a humid, subtropical climate with hot summers and wet, cool winters due to the influence of ocean currents and rainfall from monsoons.

Mountain High

The region between the Yellow River and the Yangtze River (more than 500 kilometers or 310 miles to the south) was the cradle of

A calm day on the Yellow Sea off the shore of Qingdao.

Chinese culture, agriculture, technology, and science for more than six thousand years. Historically, when the river flooded, it would wash away most villages in its path; thus, people lived high up in hills or low down near riversides to avoid floods or groundwater contamination.

The highest peak in the province is Mount Tai (also known as Taishan), one of China's five sacred mountains. Mount Tai is arguably the foremost of the holy mountains. The five sacred mountains are often regarded as the "axis of the world" in China. They are associated with long-held ideas about the origin of its culture and civilization. The mountains symbolize Chinese Taoism, a combination of philosophy and religion dating back to ancient times.

Ancient Culture

Shandong culture has felt the influence of Chinese civilization for thousands of years. For a time, Shandong was the capital of the Zhou Dynasty (1040–221 BCE) and later became the center of Buddhism in China.

Shandong is known as the birthplace of Confucius, a renowned Chinese philosopher, teacher, and politician who lived between 551-479 BCE. Confucius was the central figure of a philosophy called Confucianism, which was built on the teachings of an older ancient Chinese philosophy called Legalism. Confucius believed that people should lead a good life by conforming to the rules of society and living simply. Today, the people of this region are greatly influenced by Confucian ideals. In general, they are hard-working people who value education highly.

Visitors can climb thousands of stone steps to reach the South Gate to Heaven atop Mount Tai, Shandong's highest peak.

This scene depicts a naval battle fought during the First Opium War (1839-1842).

Watch this dramatic showcase of the cuisine of the Boshan district of Zibo, a city in central Shandong Province.

Between 1856 and 1860, several battles of the Opium Wars were fought in and around Shandong between Great Britain and China. After being ruled by Japan from 1895 to 1945, Shandong has served as a province of China since 1946. The Chinese have been good stewards over more than five thousand years with their agricultural innovations such as irrigation systems for flood control and soil enrichment. They have learned how to work with nature rather than fight against it.

OPIUM WARS

In the early 1800s, traders from Britain (and some from other countries) supplied large quantities of opium to China. Opium is the naturally occurring drug known as an opiate. Today, it is used to make the synthetic opioid, heroin, but it was a popular recreational drug in China back then. Historians estimate that about 25% of Chinese men were addicted to opium. The Chinese government tried to restrict opium trade and distribution for the better part of a century. The tipping point came in 1839 when the Chinese seized and destroyed several hundred tons of smuggled opium from British traders in Guangdong. The British eventually retaliated by attacking Canton (now Guangzhou), igniting a two-year war which they ultimately won. As part of the treaty ending the war, the British took control of Hong Kong.

Fourteen years later, tensions escalated again when the Chinese boarded a British ship and arrested its crew. The British retaliated by using a warship to shell Canton. The Chinese then burned several European warehouses in the city. A second opium war broke out, with the French joining the British in attacking China. It ended with the Europeans capturing the Chinese capital Beijing in 1860.

Between a river that flooded regularly and changing weather patterns, the geographical location has played a major role in shaping the foundation of the Shandong culture. In addition, the location's climate permits a long growing season, so there are lots of fresh vegetables available all year long, plus fish are abundant from the Yellow Sea. When you combine all these factors with a rich cultural history and a large immigrant population, you get Shandong cuisine.

Pichai Yuan is a famous food street in downtown Qingdao, a coastal city in Shandong.

Shandong Cuisine

Shandong's distinctive cuisine is strongly influenced by location, but Shandong also has a lot of sub regions with their own subcultures due to proximity to major rivers or mountains. More than 100 minority groups are living within the borders of Shandong Province. They speak different languages and dialects, which give them distinction from surrounding regions. This has had a significant impact on its cuisine.

The cuisine is heavily influenced by seafood, vegetables, seaweed, and pork, and it is known for its rich flavors and simple cooking methods. Like other regions in China, Shandong cuisine is also influenced by food culture from what is now the capital city of Beijing, which lies to the north of Shandong. Historically, Shandong was considered an essential middle station during the Tang Dynasty (618-907). It gained importance as a food supply station to provide Beijing with seafood and vegetables from Qingdao and Weihai. The transportation routes from North China were abundant enough that fresh products could be provided all year round. This established a foundation for the vegetable supplies in the Shandong Province.

Shandong is a northern province, so it has a lot of dishes that are quite different from southern dishes. Northern styles of cooking use a lot of stir-frying and specific oils to flavor food. In Shandong, they produce and use a lot of peanut oil. Its use in cooking is a large part of Shandong cuisine that sets it apart from other regional styles. Using a cooking style called *bao*, a lot of seafood, vegetables, and meat are stir-fried for a brief time over high heat with oil to create a dish that balances textures, colors, and flavors.

The province is known for its lightly flavored dishes with fresh ingredients that are cooked simply without many spices (think salt, garlic, and ginger) or strong taste combinations. Stewing, braising, and roasting are other commonly used cooking techniques. The primary goal in Shandong cooking is to feature the natural essence, color, and taste of its ingredients.

Zha Jiang Mian is a Chinese dish of ground pork over wheat noodles.

What's Cooking?

The primary ingredients of Shandong dishes are seafood (no surprise given its coastal location), pork, vinegar, vegetables, rice, and grains. The seafood in Shandong cuisine is mainly fish and shellfish, including prawns, squid, and octopus. They are marinated or cooked with vegetables. Pork is an essential meat in Northern China since it can be preserved longer than beef or lamb because of the colder climate. The types of pork used are legs, necks, and ribs; they are boiled to make soups with fresh vegetables. Vegetables common to Shandong cuisine include spinach, Chinese cabbage (*bok choy*), napa cabbage, bamboo shoots, and corn on the cob.

Grains like wheat (used to make flour for noodles) and rice are also popular staples in the region. They also use sweet potato noodles, a specialty food item that some consider unique to this area alone. Other ingredients that come into play in some dishes are blood, cow tongue, and pig ear.

Thin slices of beef are also used along with chicken to make the regionally known soupy dish called Hot Pot (*Huo Guo*). This soup has many layers of different ingredients like tomatoes, potatoes, onions, mushrooms, and Chinese cabbage that bubble after adding hot liquid into the pot to cook it quickly at high heat.

Other popular dishes include *Zha Jiang Mian* which is pork with tomato sauce noodles; Dandan Noodle Soup that uses a chili oil sauce mixed with ground pork and garnished with peanuts, pickles, and cilantro; and *Mapo Tofu* which has tofu in a spicy chili oil paste.

Celebrations and Food

One of the most universal aspects of food is that no matter what part of the world it is or what kinds of people there are, food brings people together. This is very much the case in the Chinese culture where huge national holidays are celebrated by observing customs and eating delicious food.

The Lantern Festival is one of many national celebrations across China each year.

Chapter 1: Shandong   17

The year begins with the most significant celebration, Spring Festival (Chinese New Year). In Shandong, it is a Spring Festival tradition to visit the cemetery, where family members ceremoniously burn joss paper and let off firecrackers at the graves of their ancestors. It is supposed to remind the living to bring honor to their family and treasure their time with loved ones. Not uncommon in Confucianism, this kind of ritual is designed to keep people on a good path and avoid the temptation to stray from that path.

Spring Festival is several days of lively, colorful celebration and is anchored by large family meals. For example, *sweet and sour carp* is a dish that is typically served on special occasions such as the Festival. It is perhaps the most famous dish in Shandong. The flavorful sauce combines onions, soy sauce, rice wine, sugar, pepper, and ginger. The fish is deep-fried and served crispy.

Each spring, there is a Daheyan pickle festival in Jinan where visitors can try and buy different types of pickles from all around Shandong. Local restaurants also offer unique dishes that feature these pickles, such as Braised Pork with Daheyan.

April brings the Qingming Festival (Tomb Sweeping Festival), where families visit cemeteries to sweep tombs, clean headstones, and leave offerings like fresh fruit or spirit money (paper replicas of material objects like cars or houses). During Qingming, it is a custom for people in Shandong to eat *jianbing*, a crepe-like dish made from batter and filled with other ingredients. It can be found all over China but has its origins in Shandong. It is traditionally cooked on the banks of the Yellow River during Qingming Festival where people appreciate the beauty of the flowing current while they eat their *jianbing*.

Dezhou braised chicken is a dish originating in the Qing Dynasty more than 300 years ago. Named for its city of origin, the chicken is savory, fleshy, and tender. The chicken is first marinated in a mixture of egg whites, cornstarch, salt, and soy sauce until its skin turns slightly yellow. Then, it is fried until it's well-done but not dry inside. To finish the dish, green peppers are added to a sweetened broth containing garlic chips and a few other spices. Red dates may also be added for color and flavor.

Shandong also has desserts like rice cakes and steamed, stuffed buns. The people love sweet dishes like *Tang Yuan*, small dumplings made from glutinous rice flour traditionally filled with black sesame paste. However, fillings from sweet red bean paste, peanuts, or sesame to apple or hawthorn berries are also used.

Food is an integral part of Chinese culture, and it has been for centuries. From Spring Festival to Qingming Festival celebrations, food brings people together across Shandong.

Traditional Chinese street food called jianbing.

INGREDIENTS:
mushrooms, bamboo shoots, fresh herbs, frogs, turtles, fish, shrimp, spinach, bok choy, and bean sprouts

CHAPTER 2
Anhui & Fujian

Unlike Shandong, with its primarily coastal location lending it much of its identity, the Anhui and Fujian Provinces are mountainous, a characteristic that strongly influences its people and their lives.

Anhui Province

Anhui is a landlocked province of Eastern China known for its Huangshan Mountains. The beauty of these peaks, often shrouded by low-hanging clouds, with their stark granite slopes dotted with twisted pines, has been lauded in poems and captured in paintings for centuries.

The Anhui climate is subtropical (warm and humid) with four distinct seasons. The location of the Anhui Province (and its neighbors Zhejiang and Jiangsu) is sometimes called "Jianhuai" or "Jinhua," which refers to the area along the Grand Canal constructed during the Sui Dynasty.

The Grand Canal is the longest man-made waterway in the world. It was built to carry grain and other commodities from the fertile regions in the south to the economic center of Beijing to make it easier for merchants and workers to access resources. In its heyday, it ran 3,200 kilometers from Beijing south to Hangzhou.

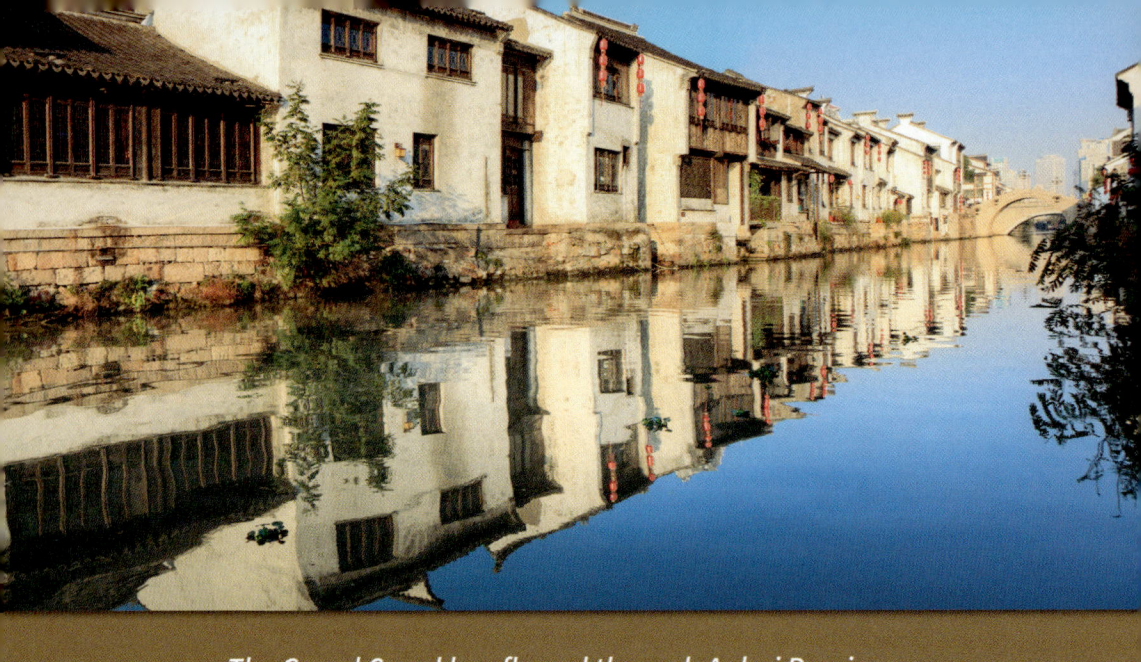

The Grand Canal has flowed through Anhui Province for more than 1,000 years.

It joins with the Yangtze River at Zhenjiang, near Nanjing, which lies on Anhui's eastern border with Jiangsu. Today, a nearly six-kilometer portion of the canal that still runs through the northeastern edge of Anhui is a UNESCO World Heritage site (designated in 2014). It has flowed uninterrupted for more than 1,000 years, playing a significant role in China's stable and prosperous economy.

A Tale of One City

The name Anhui means "peaceful beauty" and comes from a combination of the names of two of its oldest cities, Anqing and Huizhou.

Another of the province's ancient cities was Sizhou, which is famous in Chinese folklore. The story revolves around Shuimu, a demon spirit of the water. One of her favorite tricks was to bring devastating floods to Sizhou every year, which angered Yue Huang, lord of the skies. When he tried to capture Shuimu, she escaped, and in retaliation, buried Sizhou under a deluge of water large enough to form a lake.

Shuimu was later captured by the goddess Kuan-yin, who disguised herself as a noodle vendor and served Shuimu magic noodles that turned to heavy chains in her intestines. Weighted by the chains, Shuimu was dropped into a deep well at the base of a mountain to remain there for eternity.

This tale of Sizhou is a popular folk legend, but in reality, what caused the city to be flooded is unclear. One story dates back to 1128, which says the Yellow River was deliberately diverted, and major dikes were breached to form a barrier of deep water to block invaders. The most likely explanation is that the Yellow RIver naturally changed course over the centuries as parts of it became clogged with heavy silt. The water found a new course, merging with the Huai River and slowly flooding the area. Hongze Lake quadrupled in size, and the ruins of Sizhou lie remarkably preserved in its depths.

Hongze Lake was once one-quarter the size it is today, before it swelled to submerge the ancient city of Sizhou.

The Yangtzee River flows through Anqing in Southern Anhui Province.

From Rural to Modern

The history of the province is influenced by its topography. The region includes many mountains and hills, which give way to a flat alluvial plain that is well-suited for rice growing. It explains why, historically, the staple grain in this region is rice and why many people in this region are rice farmers.

Over the past century, this region has been a major player in terms of modernization and industrialization. Anhui Province was not as severely damaged during the Cultural Revolution as other areas in China, allowing it to modernize and industrialize more quickly.

The Cultural Revolution was a wide-reaching social and political campaign by the past leader of China, Mao Zedong. The 10-year campaign was launched in 1966 and sought to institute a continuous revolution among the people of China against traditional and capitalist elements. During this period, privileged urban students were forced to move to rural provinces like Anhui to work on farms. The displaced Chinese youth referred to the policy as "up to the mountains and down to the farms." The policy deprived thousands of young people of a formal education.

Colorful Culture

The region's culture has been dramatically influenced by its location along the Yangtze River, one of China's major waterways. The area shares a border with five other provinces: Hubei, Henan, Jiangsu, Zhejiang, and Shandong. This means that residents of this region have been influenced by the cultures of these provinces in addition to their own.

One of the most expressive examples of Anhui culture is Nuo Opera. A popular folk opera in many parts of the country, Anhui Nuo is unique because it has developed independently over thousands of years. Nuo Opera is still performed on Anhui's traditional opera stages and attracts an enthusiastic following across the province.

In Nuo Opera, the players wear ferocious and colorful masks.

The original purpose of Nuo Opera was to repel evil spirits. Nuo Opera clans are now popular tourist attractions, performing for tourists from all over the world. Performers wear ferocious masks with colorful outfits and sing with a high-pitched, shrill voice. The plots are complex and deep with meaning. The performers sing in dialects specific to different regions of Anhui.

In Anhui, the most famous Nuo Opera is found in Chizhou, in the southern part of the province. Chizhou Nuo is learned through oral tradition, not written scripts. Nuo plays are generally based on historical events or famous stories of heroic deeds by the Anhui people. The most exciting part of any play is the climax when Nuo characters fight off evil spirits with drums and cymbals.

Scan here to take a soaring tour around Anhui Province.

Revelers wash away the bad luck of the past year during the Water Splashing Festival.

Anhui Cuisine

The long-term residence of many ethnic groups such as the Han Chinese, Hui Chinese, Mongolians, Manchus, and Koreans has had a significant impact not only on the culture but also on the cuisine. There are a large number of local food ingredients and resources available. The region's cuisine consists of flavors from sweet and salty to sour and pungent.

    A wide range of cooking styles is used in this region, including some from abroad, such as those from Japan, Thailand, Italy, France, and England. The flavoring options are also very diverse due to all the different cultures that have influenced the cuisine.

    Festivals and celebrations are a big part of the culture in this region. One event is the Water Splashing Festival where water is thrown at people in an attempt to wash away the bad luck of the past year and to encourage good luck for the new year.

Food plays a big part in these traditions and celebrations, especially those food items associated with luck and fortune. Some of these include:

- Dumplings and glutinous rice balls
- Long noodles (representing long life)
- Fish (for abundance and prosperity)
- Eggs (symbolizing the sun which brings light and warmth to the Earth; also, for happiness and good luck)

Other festivals that have food as a key part of their traditions include the Qingming Festival, where families visit ancestral

During Qingming Festival, it is customary to burn symbolic paper representing money ancestors can use in the afterlife.

Raw bamboo shoots like these are chopped into small slices to be used as a popular ingredient in Anhui cuisine.

gravesites and burn paper money for them to use in the afterlife. Then, they eat dishes such as dumplings or fish to symbolize a rich harvest.

Wild Life

In Anhui, the people focus on using wild ingredients such as mushrooms, bamboo shoots, and especially herbs from the mountains for their cooking instead of domesticated crops. They also cook a lot of wild-caught mountain game, along with frogs, turtles, fish, and small shrimp.

Controlling cooking temperatures and time are necessary skills in good Anhui cooking. Varying the degree of heat applied to the food with precision, depending on the characteristics of the ingredients and the desired flavor of the given dish, is the key to a good outcome.

Anhui has three regional cooking styles, which are defined by the Huai River region in the north, the centrally located Yangtze River region, and the Yellow Mountain region in the south, which has the most well-known Anhui style.

In the north, one of the best-known dishes is *Bagongshan dou fu* (Bagongshan bean curd). This dish is made with boiled tofu cut into cubes, then rolled and deep-fried to be golden and crispy outside but tender inside. Stir-fried bamboo shoots, mushrooms, onions, and garlic are added. The dish is then braised in a sauce often made with soy sauce, rice wine, and sugar.

People in the Yangtze River region love *Luzhou roast duck*, which is roasted with a coating of malt sugar. Although not as well known worldwide as Peking duck, *Luzhou roast duck* is a respected dish not only in Anhui but across China.

Nestled in the Yellow Mountains to the south is the Huizhou district, where a popular snack is *Xie ke huang*, which translates as "crab shell yellow." This is a small pastry in the shape of a crab shell. However, *Xie ke huang* does not necessarily contain any crab at all, although it may. The pastries can be sweet or savory and are filled with anything from pork and crab to sweet bean paste and dates. Traditionally, they are wrapped in sesame then oven-baked to a crispy golden hue (this is typically a yellowish color, which explains the name).

Anhui is one of the most fascinating regions in China. The cuisine has been influenced by its location, history, and culture over time. From wild ingredients to local food resources used for cooking styles, flavors, and dishes, this region offers a diverse culinary experience.

Fujian

About 700 kilometers (435 miles) to the south of Anhui lies another province whose cuisine is influenced by its mountainous terrain.

Fujian is a province on the southeast coast of mainland China and the Taiwan Strait. The region is known for its beautiful natural landscapes, including lowlands with orchards, gentle streams, and tea gardens in the east and expansive mountains with steep cliffs in the west. The Wuyi Mountains rise up to 6,000 feet (about 1,800 meters), imposing a natural barrier between Fujian and the rest of the country stretching out to the west.

The Wuyi Mountains make for striking scenery in northern Fujian Province.

History and Culture

Historically, the region was home to several small kingdoms until China unified imperial control in 221 BCE. Twelve hundred years later, in the mid-900s, shortly after the fall of the Tang Dynasty, it was divided again into two states: Yin in the north and Min in the south. During this time, the region gained economic significance by producing silk, iron, paper, and ink. By the mid-13th century, it became politically unified as Fujian Province under Mongol rule. The famous Italian explorer Marco Polo visited the city of Fuzhou on the northeast coast of Fujian in the late 1200s. He later wrote of the abundance of ginger and of powerful South China tigers. Now extinct in the wild, they roamed the area freely at that time.

In 1644, the Mongols were defeated by the Chinese Ming Dynasty. Fujian became one of the most important maritime provinces. As a seafaring region with strong ties to Taiwan, Fujian has experienced all of China's regime changes over time: from Imperial to Nationalist

Rebels at Shanghai.

The Taiping Rebellion was a 14-year civil war and one of the darkest times in Chinese history.

to Communist control. Today, the region has a population of nearly 39 million people and is ranked third in terms of economic output behind Shanghai and Zhejiang Province.

The regional culture of Fujian is based partly upon Cantonese and Taiwanese influences, with Fujian people having strong connections with merchants in coastal cities. There have been many wars over time that have impacted the culture, such as the

Taiping Rebellion, a massive civil war that raged across the country for 13 years from 1851 to 1864, and the First and Second Opium Wars (1840-1842, 1856-1860).

Fujian Cuisine

Its history, culture, and location have influenced the food of Fujian. The cuisine is mainly rice-based, with seafood coming from the coastal areas. Fujian cuisine is known for its emphasis on matching flavors and using cooking techniques to bring out the best in dishes.

In terms of ingredients, rice is used in most dishes which usually consist of pork, chicken, or eggs. Vegetables are also present in most dishes, with popular vegetables being leafy greens like spinach, bok choy, and bean sprouts.

CALIFORNIA DREAMING

The California Gold Rush is the name given to the period from 1848 to 1855 when tens of thousands of people from around the world rushed to Northern California after gold was discovered in the developing region. The fortune seekers were mainly from America, but thousands also came from the Sandwich Islands (present-day Hawaii), Peru, Mexico, Chile, and China.

Most of the Chinese prospectors were from Guangdong and Fujian Provinces, as they were close to Hong Kong, a major port from which ships would leave for America. The region at the time was embroiled in a series of bloody conflicts, and many men were looking to escape hopeless circumstances in their war-ravaged homeland

The food of Fujian is also influenced by specific local ingredients, such as fish (freshwater and marine) and different kinds of mushrooms and fungi. Other popular ingredients and resources include:

- pork (bacon, ribs, liver)
- chicken (fried or boiled)
- eggs (boiled, stir-fried with vegetables, or in omelets)
- various local seafood and seasonings (especially in coastal areas)
- vegetables (like spinach, bok choy, and bean sprouts), fungi, and mushrooms)

In addition to food, Fujian is also known for its diverse styles of cooking. One example is the Shanghai-style, in which ingredients are not marinated or seasoned with spices beforehand. Instead, soy sauce, salt, and sugar are used to season the food during the cooking process.

Another type of cuisine is Hakka cuisine, in which dishes are usually served in individual bowls instead of the typical family-style dining; other styles include Teochew and Northern styles.

Traditional Dishes

The region of Fujian is known for many traditions, holidays, celebrations, and rites of passage. Some of the most important festivals are the annual Qingming Festival in early April and the Moon Festival, which takes place in mid-autumn each year. As in all big Chinese celebrations, food plays a significant role during these festivities. It symbolizes bringing harmony and happiness to families and friends.

In Fuzhou, the capital city of Fujian, the traditional food that people eat during the Qingming Festival is *Bobo Kueh* or *Qingming Kueh*. Its unique feature is the use of bobo grass. The bobo grass is squeezed, producing a juice mixed with glutinous rice milk, then kneaded to make kueh skins. The bobo grass juice gives the skins a

A spread of Hakka cuisine dishes shown just before being served.

deep green color. They are then wrapped around fillings such as radish or red bean paste.

Another favorite Fujian dish is *Fotiaoqiang*, or as it is more commonly known, Buddha Jumps Over the Wall. This name means that the dish is so good, even the strong-willed and vegetarian Buddha himself would be so tempted he would leap over a wall to get it. The dish is a complex shark fin soup that takes days to prepare. Other ingredients include quail eggs, yellow wine, chicken, pork, mushrooms, ginseng, scallops, and abalone, to name a few.

Fujian is a region that has been heavily influenced by its history and culture. This has resulted in many different cooking styles in this region, all involving ingredients and techniques that bring out the best in its dishes.

INGREDIENTS:
chili peppers, peppercorns, ginger, garlic, scallions, rice wine, black vinegar, sweet potato, shallots, garlic, and cinnamon

CHAPTER 3

Sichuan & Hunan

The landlocked provinces of Sichuan and Hunan are located in the middle-western part of Southern China. This area includes cities like Chengdu, Sichuan's capital, and Huwaihua, the largest city in Hunan. Sichuan and Hunan are separated by Guizhou Province to the south and Chongqing Municipality to the north. The region has four provincial-level divisions: Sichuan, Hubei, Guizhou, and Hunan, and one municipality: Chongqing.

    The climate can be very harsh and dry, especially in the north of Sichuan, where cold winds are common. The western part of the province is also very mountainous, which can make farming difficult at times. However, this region does feature some beautiful lakes and lush vegetation. Mountains surround this region on three sides, making it prone to earthquakes that have historically caused significant damage throughout the region.

Rich History and Culture

Chengdu is considered to be one of China's literary centers. Sichuan's capital has produced giants of historical literature from the Tang, Ming, and Song dynasties. Notable modern writers Ba JIn and Guo Moruo also hail from Chengdu.

Patrons line up as they wait to enter a library in Chengdu, a city that is known as one of China's great literary centers.

Chili peppers are a staple ingredient of Sichuan and Hunan cooking.

Over time, the region's culture has changed from a traditional way of life revolving around agriculture toward an industrially developed society. Since land reforms after 1949, when Mao Zedong came into power, much land was taken away from large, prosperous farms (called "people's communes") and given back to individual farmers. This created an incentive for people to make their own money instead of relying on the government.

Mao was actually a native of Hunan. He was born in Shaoshan in 1893. Decades before becoming Chairman Mao, leader of the communist government in China, Mao was the son of a wealthy landowner and grew up working on his father's farm in Hunan.

One custom of the Hunan culture is known as the Shefan dinner. On Chunse, the fifth day after the beginning of spring, men in Western Hunan repair their plowing tools for the spring planting season, while women and children pick baskets full of fresh mountain tarragon and shallots. These ingredients are essential for a She dinner, which is observed late on the afternoon of Chunse. The tarragon is mixed with

Stewed Chicken with Three Cups of Sauce is a traditional Hunan dish.

pieces of bacon and peanuts, which are then folded into sticky rice and served with meat and vegetables.

The history of the culture and its location have greatly informed the cuisine of Sichuan and Hunan today. People there have been influenced by nearby regions that they tried to emulate and improve upon. The nearby region of Guangdong (Canton) had a significant influence on the Hunan area since it was so close and easy to get to. This is why there are so many Cantonese influences in the food of Hunan. A prominent cooking style used in Hunan is stewing. Stewed dishes often include *la jiao*, which is red chili paste made from scratch. It can be used as a thickener for any sauce you want to make.

Another nearby region that has influenced this cuisine is Jiangxi, which sits next to Hunan to the east, so it is not surprising that they have similar food cultures. Traditional dishes here include spicy marinated pork and *Stewed Chicken with Three Cups of Sauce.* There are also the cuisines of Dongbei and Shandong to the north which contribute different techniques as well.

Spicy Cuisine

The cuisine of Sichuan and Hunan is traditionally based on rice with some vegetables, fish, or meat. Both regions are known for easy access to ingredients such as ginger, garlic, chili peppers (and others) which all grow well there. Thus, these spices are easily added to many dishes. A well-known local saying goes:

"Sichuan people don't fear spiciness. Hunan people fear there is no spiciness."

Sichuan, famous around the country and the world for spicy food, uses *numbing spice (málà),* which means the spice level in Sichuan cooking both burns and numbs the tongue simultaneously. Hunan likes it spicy as well;

HOT TO BE COOL

Are you having trouble cooling down on a hot day? Try some Hunan chicken! It may sound strange but eating spicy food can help the body cool down. That's because the body's natural reaction to the heat of spicy food is to start sweating. Sweating is the body's way of cooling itself. This will only work in environments with low humidity, however. Dry air allows sweat to evaporate. In humid air, you would just get sweaty.

What if you're just trying to cool your mouth down during a spicy meal? Cold water might feel good going down, but it won't do much for the fire in your mouth. Capsaicin, the chemical in peppers that causes them to be spicy, is not water-soluble, so water won't dilute it. What you need is something with fat in it. Whole milk, for example, would help as capsaicin is soluble in fat. Or try mixing some sour cream or yogurt in with that spicy chicken. That should work...no sweat.

some say even spicier than Sichuan. Using lots of fresh chili peppers and plenty of cooking oil, food is cooked in a "dry hot" style, which is seriously spicy.

The use of málà is characteristic of Sichuan cuisine. This typical Sichuan seasoning is made by boiling Sichuan peppercorns and chili peppers together with soy sauce and vinegar, cooking wine or sherry, various spices such as ginger and garlic, and using this mixture to marinate the meat before stir-frying it. It also uses plenty of chopped green onions (which appear in most recipes) and occasionally ginger. Sichuan cuisine is known for its combination of spicy, sweet, and sour flavors, commonly referred to as *málà* flavors.

The two main types of chili peppers are the red ones, which are hot and spicy, and the green ones, which are less spicy. The green chili peppers are used more in Hunan cuisine, where they are pickled or even fermented into a sauce known as *Pixian Douban*.

It isn't all about the chilis when it comes to ingredients from these regions. In Sichuan, you will typically find liberal amounts of *douchi* (fermented black beans), rice wine, black vinegar, and sweet potato noodles (also called glass noodles). In Hunan, it is green onions, shallots, garlic, ginger, spicy oil, and cinnamon.

Douchi, *which is a compound of salty, fermented black beans, is used as an ingredient in many Sichuan dishes.*

Take a look at some of the events and traditions surrounding China's Dragon Boat Festival.

Common cooking techniques used in Sichuan and Hunan China include stir-frying, braising, steaming, and smoking. Stir-fry techniques are very common, using a large amount of oil that is maintained at high heat for a long time. Braising gives meat a unique flavor after being seared then simmered with vegetables, spices, and other ingredients until they have been fully cooked and then placed in vessels of clay or clay-like materials called brick pots.

Steaming is done by placing food on top of a plate that is in turn placed on top of a pot filled with boiling water then covering the whole thing. This cooking technique preserves the flavor and makes leaves, root vegetables, or seafood taste especially good due to the resulting intensified natural flavors. Finally, smoking is done by hanging meats over fire pits that are first lined with fragrant plants like rosemary or thyme, which gives the meat a more complex flavor.

Chapter 3: Sichuan & Hunan

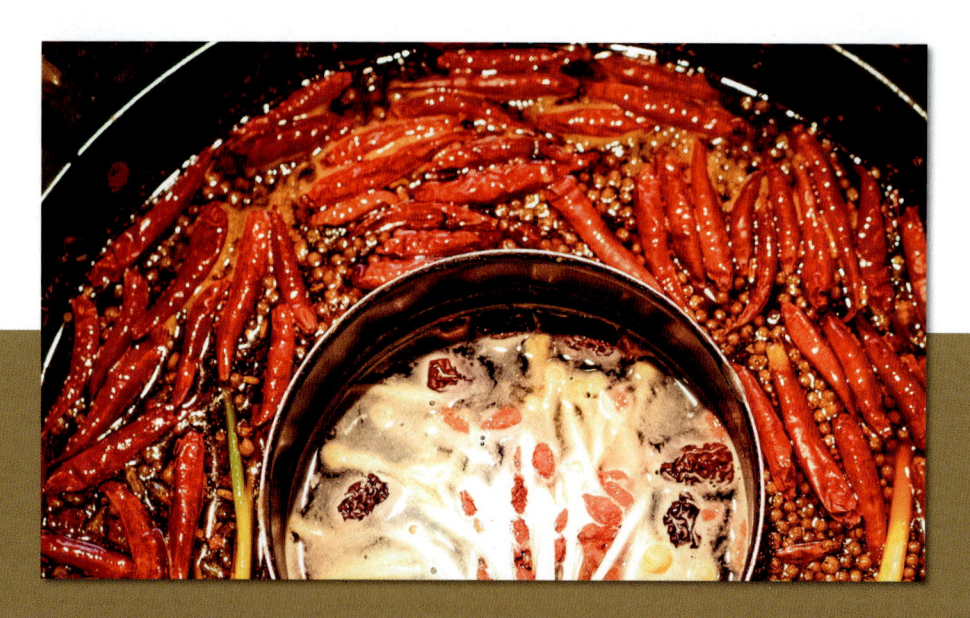

Huo Guo is a traditional Sichuan comfort food.

Celebrating with Food

The Sichuan and Hunan regions of China both share a unique cuisine that is spicy, rich, and influenced by many different cultures that have historically moved into the area. Countries such as Mongolia, Tibet, and India were all influential on these regions due to their proximity. The best way for people in this region to communicate with each other was through food, so these cultures brought new flavors and techniques along with them while also influencing the local ingredients used throughout both provinces. A strong sense of culture can be felt here because families often hold banquets for family members who have passed away on Tomb Sweeping Day (Qingming Festival). They believe eating certain foods such as abalone and frog will bring good luck to their family in the new year. In Sichuan, hot pot is a must for the Chinese New Year, as it represents prosperity and growth.

    Practically, a Sichuan hot pot, or *Huo Guo*, can contain almost anything that a hearty broth and soup would have. Traditionally, it is a blend of Sichuan peppercorns, dried chilis, and spices (think cardamom, star anise, fennel, and cumin) combined with wine and chicken stock to make a base. Then, scallions, ginger, garlic, and lemongrass are added to the bubbling concoction before people gather around to dip in items such as meat, seafood, quail eggs, and mushrooms to be cooked fondue-style.

The Dragon Boat Festival is celebrated around the country but has its origins in Hunan legend. As the story goes, on the fifth day of the fifth month in 278 BCE, a poet named Qu Yuan drowned in the Miluo River. People who lived along the river took to their boats in search of the body which was never found. Each year on that same date, it is the custom for people to fill sections of bamboo with rice and row out onto local rivers to toss them into the water as an offering to Qu Yuan.

In Hunan, the food that people enjoy during the Dragon Boat Festival is called *zongzi*. *Zongzi* are dumplings made of glutinous rice traditionally stuffed with a savory pork filling wrapped in bamboo leaves and boiled.

The famous dish from Sichuan is *Mapo Doufu*. This is a soup-like dish made with a combination of red-hot chili oil, soft tofu, fermented chili bean paste, ground meat (beef or pork), and Sichuan peppercorns. *Mapo Doufu* can be served in various ways, including on top of rice or with noodles.

Dong an zi ji (Dong'an chicken) is the best-known poultry dish from Hunan. It is simply chicken flavored with chili and clear rice vinegar and is named from the county it is believed to have come from. Like any old Chinese dish, it comes with a legend. The story tells of traveling merchants looking for something to eat late in the day. They came upon a restaurant run by three old ladies. But as it is nearly time to close, the kitchen was bare. The women, however, took pity on the travelers, went out back, slaughtered some chickens, flavored the meat with whatever seasoning they had handy, and called it a dish. The happy merchants spread the word of the delicious creation far and wide.

Other famous dishes from Sichuan and Hunan include Kung Pao chicken, *Hong Shao Rou* (braised pork belly), and Dandan noodles.

Although the flavors, ingredients, and cooking techniques have changed over time due to foreign influence, the regions of Sichuan and Hunan have managed to maintain their unique culture and embrace the history of their rich culinary tradition.

INGREDIENTS:
fish, oysters, shrimp, crab, rice, pork, beef, mutton, green onion, ginger root, garlic, red pepper flakes, five-spice powder, black pepper, sesame oil, and chicken

CHAPTER 4

Zhejiang, Jiangsu & Guangdong

Zhejiang is an affluent coastal province on the southeastern coast of the country. It borders Jiangsu and Anhui to the north, Jiangxi to the west, Fujian to the south, and the East China Sea. Across the Qiantang River to its northeast lies Shanghai. The provincial capital city is Hangzhou.

Jiangsu, also known as Lower Yangtze, is the province immediately north of Zhejiang. It is located along China's Yellow Sea coast near Shanghai and Nanjing and has a population of 114 million (approximately 8% of China's total population).

As Old as Time

Like many other Chinese regions, the Zhejiang-Jiangsu region also has a rich history that has included the rule of feudal dynasties. The region was settled by the native Yue people at least 8,000 years ago. About 2,000 years ago, they were conquered by northern tribes known as Qin. The Qin Dynasty reigned over the land that now forms both provinces for almost two hundred years until 202 BCE when Liu Bang founded the Han Dynasty, which ruled China until 220 CE. After this point, China split into three separate states. Then after briefly uniting once again under one empire between 960-1127, it was divided by competing warlords through much of the 13th century.

The cultural changes that occurred during the long period of division between warlords in this region primarily occurred when invaders took control of the area. This caused many people to flee to other regions, reinforcing local populations with new waves of immigrants and causing lots of cultural mixing wherever they went. Even though foreign rule wasn't always kinder in this region than in other parts of China, the provinces were still a major trading center. When foreign powers ruled over much of China, even though they were also invading and conquering many different regions, life was especially difficult for locals in Zhejiang and Jiangsu.

After the Opium War in 1842, many of the European countries took over China's coastal regions as part of the treaty agreement to end the fighting. In 1864, the British invaded Shanghai, which was the most important and largest city in China and made it a free trade zone. In 1895, during the Sino-Japanese War, China was defeated, and Japan gained control of the region from China. From 1927 to 1949, this region was under the control of Chiang Kai-shek and his

Rising from the banks of the Qiantang River, Hangzhou is the capital of Zhejiang Province.

Kuomintang government. In 1949, Mao Zedong and his Communists took control of both Jiangsu and Zhejiang Provinces.

In 1978, a man named Deng Xiaoping came into power and changed things in this region by giving economic growth a higher priority than ideological purity, which allowed for more outside influences to come into the area. Today, this region has undergone many changes since Deng implemented more inclusive policies.

Mao was Chairman of the Communist Party of China from 1943 to 1976.

High-End Culture

Kunqu Opera is an art form that originated in Jiangsu Province. It combines elements of Beijing Opera with plays from the old tradition of Shanting Opera. Kunqu is noted for its sad lyrics and slow, mournful melodies.

In Zhejiang, the people speak many dialects of Wu. There are two main dialects, Taizhou and Xiantong. Mandarin is now a common second language in Zhejiang.

Jiangsu has a mix of Han and Chuang people, with accents from the north and south. In addition, a dialect called Fuzhou is spoken by the local population. Moreover, a form of Minnan language is also spoken in Dongtai, a city in Jiangsu. The biggest minority group in the province is the Manchu people, who speak a language known as Manchurian or Standard Mandarin.

Zhejiang and Jiangsu have a history of prosperity. In the 14th century, both regions were centers of trade and industry as well as significant cultural activity. A new style of performance art called Pingshu emerged from this time. This combination of singing, storytelling, and poetry is still popular today.

Zhejiang and Jiangsu are both affluent regions in China with a strong business tradition. Today, the region is seen as a center for manufacturing and processing food, but it was once known for its silk culture along with its tea production.

Seafood Surplus

The history, culture, and location all inform the cuisine of the region. To begin with, Zhejiang Province is known for its seafood dishes. One reason for this is that it borders Hangzhou Bay which provides access to the East China Sea.

The Chinese storytelling art called Pingshu is often performed in small rooms like this one.

In China, small plate dishes like these buns are known as xiaochi.

    Jiangsu's coastline is on the Yellow Sea, a source of fish and crustaceans such as oysters, shrimp, and crabs. As such, seafood is a major part of Jiangsu cuisine as well.

    The second main ingredient in both Jiangsu and Zhejiang cuisine is rice because it grows well in these regions due to an abundant water supply. As noted, and expected of coastal provinces, fish plays a significant role in their cuisines, but so do pork, beef, mutton, and chicken.

    The region is also known for *xiaochi* (small eats) which are snacks like deep-fried wontons, spring rolls, glutinous rice dumplings with soup inside, rice cakes stuffed with meat or vegetables, steamed buns, and soups.

Chapter 4: Zhejiang, Jiangsu & Guangdong

Cooking Styles

The flavors of the Zhejiang and Jiangsu region are known for their light and delicate taste. The region is also known for its wide range of cooking techniques, including:

- Smoking: i.e., smoking a duck to give it a rich flavor
- Braising: a popular style for a dish like spare ribs
- Stir-frying: a quick way to cook, for example, strips of beef with spices or vegetables
- Stewing: i.e., stewing pork with seasonings
- Steaming: i.e., steaming dumplings or buns

Celebration and Food

In Zhejiang and Jiangsu, people like to celebrate big national holidays just like the rest of the country. But when it comes to the Mid-Autumn Festival, there is a local origin story.

ALL THE TEA IN CHINA

Well, not all the tea in China comes from Zhejiang, just a lot of it. The province is the largest tea producer in the country, and no country produces more tea than China. Zhejiang's wet, subtropical climate is perfect for tea production. Zhejiang University in Hangzhou offers a degree in Tea Science, and the national Tea Museum is located in the province, naturally. Zhejiang is said by experts to grow the best green tea in the world. Varieties include Longjing (the champagne of tea), Chun Lu, and Anji White.

Tourists play red lantern riddle games at Huishanmen Square in Wuxi City, Jiangsu Province during the annual Mid-Autumn Festival.

    Zhu Yuanzhang was a rebel commander in the mid-14th century. He was based in Jiangsu (in Nanjing), directing the fight against the Yuan Dynasty. Zhu faced a dilemma as intense Yuan raids made it difficult for his messengers to get through with his orders. One of his strategists came up with a plan to hide messages in harmless-seeming mooncakes. The messages told the rebel supporters to rise up on August 15th. When that night came, so did a coordinated rebel attack and a victory for Zhu. In recognition of victory, he decreed that everyone receive mooncakes.

    Mooncakes are still enjoyed at the Mid-Autumn Festival today, but the festival is commonly referred to as the Moon Festival. Mooncakes are small round pastries made from sweetened wheat

Chapter 4: Zhejiang, Jiangsu & Guangdong   53

Shenzhen is a modern city of more than 12 million people in Southern Guangdong. It connects the mainland to Hong Kong.

flour and filled with lotus seed paste, bean paste, or duck egg yolk. They are then baked to a golden brown and usually served with tea.

One of the most popular dishes in Jiangsu is Yangzhou fried rice. Dating back 1,500 years to the Sui Dynasty, this classic dish has the works: egg, mushrooms, peas, sea cucumbers, crab meat, and bamboo shoots. Today, people also like to add ingredients such as scallions, ham, or shrimp.

In Zhejiang, a strong representation of the region's bountiful seafood dishes is *Song Sao*, or West Lake Vinegar Fish in English. Cooked without oil to preserve its natural flavor, this freshwater fish is cooked sweet-and-sour style. When done well, it comes out tender with a glistening brown hue.

Guangdong

The Guangdong region is one of the most famous food regions in the world. It is the home of Cantonese cuisine. While it is

1,000 kilometers (650 miles) away from Jiangsu and Zhejiang in distance, the regions are close together in the sense that Cantonese cuisine also generally features sweet and light flavors.

Guangdong is one of the three administrative provinces in Southern China. The regional capital and provincial seat is Guangzhou. The region has a population of 100 million people, and it covers an area of more than 141,600 square kilometers (87,986 square miles). Guangdong borders Hunan Province to the north, and Fujian Province to the east, with the bustling metropolises of Macau and Hong Kong close by to the south. The Pearl River Delta is located in this region, which includes Guangzhou city at its center.

Guangdong is a coastal province, and most of its land is flat. It has a subtropical climate, and the coastal regions usually have mild winters, while the inland areas of the province are typically much colder during winter with occasional snowfall. The monsoon season runs from April to September and produces extremely humid conditions that often result in typhoons coming off the South China Sea. The region's main crops include rice, sorghum, peanut, and sesame, which thrive in the flat and warm conditions. Other resources include seafood, salt, lumber, and stone.

History & Culture

The Guangdong region is a culturally rich area with a long history of trading and cultural exchange. The major ethnic group in this region is the Han Chinese, who have been living there for thousands of years. The Han people in this region speak a dialect called Yue, or Cantonese, one of the most commonly spoken Chinese dialects in the world. Other ethnic groups included in this region are Zhuang and Miao minorities, and Hui and other Muslim people who immigrated from places like Fujian and Yunnan Provinces.

The regional culture has changed over time with the various dynasties that have ruled through the centuries. For instance, Guangdong was first ruled by the Qin Dynasty around 210 BCE. It thrived under the Han Dynasty for 400 years, embraced the

A wide view of the China Import and Export Fair, the largest trade fair in Asia, in Guangzhou, Guangdong. This province is the largest goods trader in the country.

flourishing of literature under the brief rule of the Sui Dynasty, and prospered under Tang rule in the 7th and 8th centuries.

The region has come a long way in modern times, now boasting one of the largest economies in the world, one that is bigger than the economy of all but nine other entire countries. Riding an economic boom that started in the 1990s, Guangdong is now China's largest importer and exporter of goods.

Culturally, an area known as Chaoshan in Eastern Guangdong has its own thriving identity. The people speak an ancient dialect that is challenging even for other Chinese to learn. It is known for its Chaozhou string music, in which musicians perform using several types of two-stringed lutes. Choashan also has unique dishes, such as *bak chor mee* (boiled dried noodles in sauce) and *chai tau kueh* (a savory cake stir-fried in soy sauce and garlic). However, in Guangdong, Cantonese food is the showstopper.

The Guangdong region has an extensive history of food preparation and culinary techniques. The famous three-sectioned cooking pot, the *wok*, is believed to have come from this region in around 900 BCE. Cantonese cuisine has many influences, including everything from the Wu people who came to Guangdong from Central China to other Southeast Asia and European traders.

Cooking Styles & Flavors

Cantonese cuisine is rich in flavor, freshness, and color. The region is also known for its soy sauces, black vinegar, and pickled vegetables. Food in this region tends to be healthier than other native cuisines, as many dishes are steamed with minimal oil, and flavors tend to emerge due to simmering rather than roasting or deep frying. Other cooking techniques of Guangdong are essential for flavor development in the dishes, and they include stir-frying, boiling, baking, braising, and sautéing.

Steaming is an essential Cantonese cooking style, used to create dishes such as Steamed Noodles with Pork Ribs.

One of the most common ingredients in Cantonese cuisine is rice noodles. These noodles are made with rice flour, water, and salt. Another ingredient in Cantonese cuisine is soy sauce, used in many different dishes to add flavor. Other common ingredients include green onion, ginger root, garlic, red pepper flakes, five-spice powder, black pepper, and sesame oil.

One common ingredient used in Cantonese cuisine that is not as well known is white pepper. White pepper has a different flavor than black pepper and can be a little more expensive. It is used in Cantonese cuisine because it goes well with the sweetness of some dishes.

White pepper is an ingredient often found in Cantonese recipes.

Scan here for a quick hit of the highlights of Cantonese cuisine.

Food Traditions & Festivals

Many traditional events are celebrated in the Guangdong region, including *Yu Lan*, the Hungry Ghosts Festival. The 15th day of the seventh month marks the beginning of the period where troubled spirits are believed to be roaming free. The custom is to ceremonially burn items to appease them. These items are typically paper representations of something valuable that the spirits can use when they return to the afterlife, such as money, electronics, clothing, or even fast food. People also set up altars in their homes, adorned with three cups of tea, three bowls of rice, and three pairs of chopsticks for the hungry ghosts.

The festival begins, however, by honoring ancestors with a large family meal, and the dish that revelers like to eat when they get to be as hungry as the ghosts is *peng kway*. This is a dish of rice cakes that are encased in glutinous skin. The skin is dyed bright pink (for luck) and filled with stir-fried rice, peanuts, garlic, and shallots.

Chapter 4: Zhejiang, Jiangsu & Guangdong

A blend of savory seasonings and slow roasting gives char siu a rich flavor.

Famous Dishes

The term *dim sum* refers to a range of small plate dishes typically served for lunch (and sometimes breakfast). Cantonese cooking is known for delicious *dim sum*, and among the most famous of these dishes is *zhaliang*. These are fried dough dumplings wrapped in rice noodles and sprinkled with sesame and soy or hoisin sauce. *Shuma* (pork-filled dumplings with an open-top) is another example of a popular *dim sum* dish.

Another popular Cantonese dish is *char siu*, pork that has been deeply marinated then slow roasted. It is seasoned with star anise, rice wine, and soy sauce.

Guangdong has a rich history and culture that is uniquely its own. The geography of the region and its proximity to other countries have influenced its people and their cuisine throughout time.

Dim Sum *is a globally popular type of Cantonese-style cuisine.*

Chapter 4: Zhejiang, Jiangsu & Guangdong

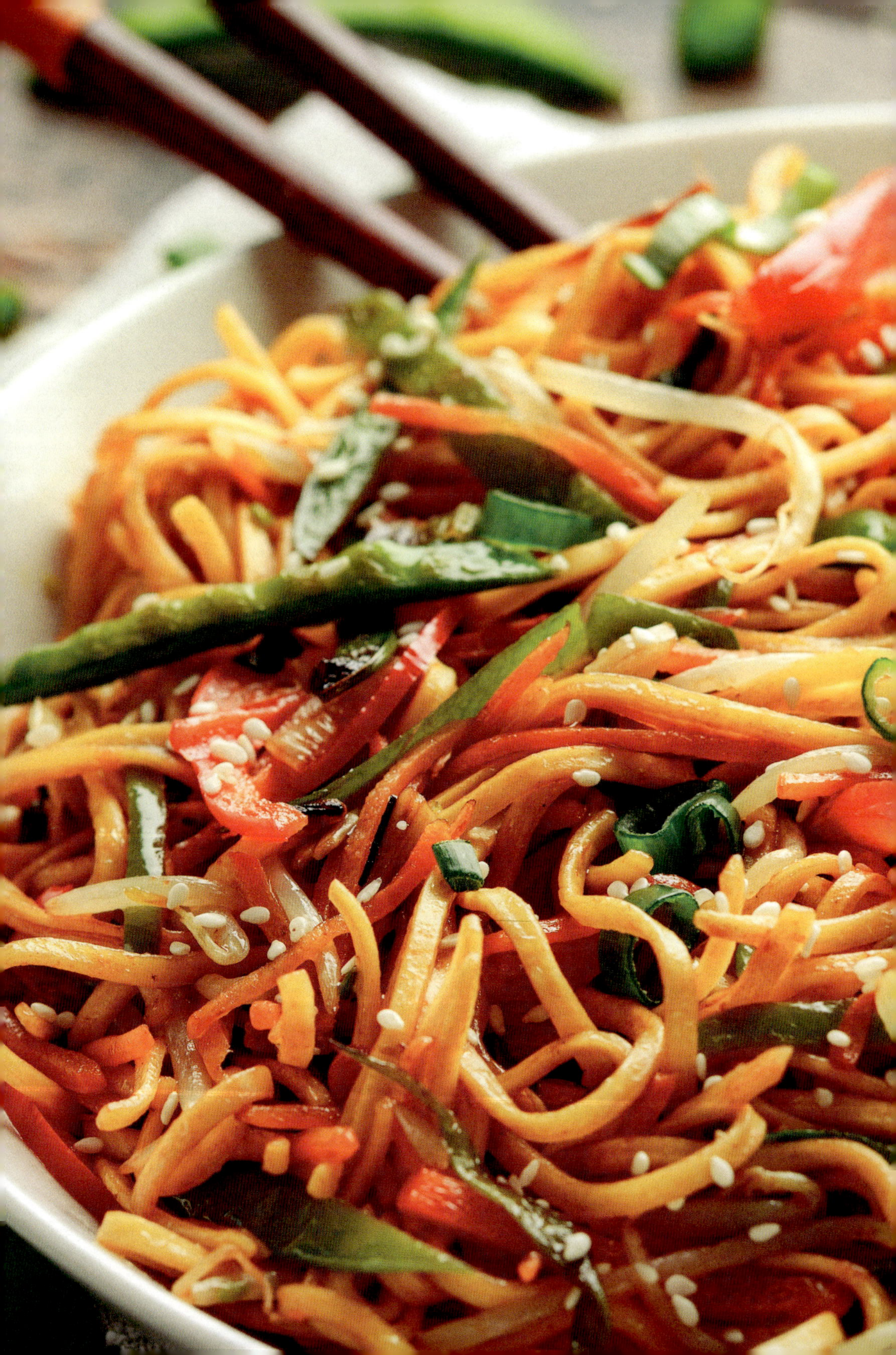

CHAPTER 5
Chinese Food in America

Chinese food in America is a culinary tradition that has been evolving for more than 100 years. In this time, the cuisine of China has become an integral part of American culture, and today, Chinese restaurants can be found in all major cities and many smaller towns across the country, offering a wide variety of styles and dishes.

When experts are asked which city has the best Chinese food in America, the three that are most likely to be named are San Francisco, Los Angeles, and New York.

San Francisco

The primary reason that San Francisco is home to excellent Chinese food is that its relative proximity to China made it an ideal destination for Chinese immigrants. Many immigrants arrived in San Francisco after the California Gold Rush in the mid-1800s.

The Gold Rush happened after news spread that a mill owner had discovered gold deposits on land near Sacramento in Northern California. More than 300,000 people flocked to the area seeking their fortune. This included about 25,000 immigrants from China, mainly from Guangdong. Of course, most of them did not strike it rich, but many stayed in America, settling in San Francisco. They were primarily single men who needed work and ended up as cooks and restaurateurs almost by default.

Today, there are now nearly half a million Chinese Americans in the San Francisco Bay area. The Chinatown neighborhood established in San Francisco after the Gold Rush is now the largest of its kind outside of Asia. It is home to dozens of restaurants like Hang Ah, which opened in 1920 and is now the oldest *dim sum* restaurant in America.

New York

Across the continent, New York City, unlike San Francisco, did not have a huge influx of immigrants after the Gold Rush. In fact, by 1873, there were only about 500 Chinese immigrants in New York.

AN INSTITUTION

Sam Wo Restaurant opened in San Francisco in 1907. The century-old noodle shop is one of the most famous in the country. It is known for its *Chow-Fun* (stir-fried beef with rice noodles and bean sprouts), a popular midnight snack. Built in the aftermath of the 1906 San Francisco earthquake, Sam Wo is now run by 3rd-generation chef-owner David Ho. Open until 3 a.m., it is famous for its "you get what you get" (read "rude") service and use of a dumbwaiter to deliver food to its upper floors.

New York City has the largest Chinese population of any city outside of Asia.

By the 1870s, however, Chinese immigrants started flocking to New York. This is when its current Chinatown neighborhood formed, though back then, it was basically just the block between Doyers, Mott, and Pell Streets. These early immigrants came from various places. Some did come east after failing to find gold in California. Others arrived in New York harbor, these mostly tradesmen looking to get away from the wide range of political unrest that was happening after a bloody civil war back home. They wanted better economic prospects for themselves and their families. Then, there were the laborers who had hired on as cheap labor to build sections of railroads across the country.

Chinatown grew over the decades, but the Chinese immigrant population stagnated when a bigoted law called the Chinese Exclusion Act passed in 1882, banning all Chinese from entering the United States. It would be more than 80 years before immigration restrictions against the Chinese people were lifted. When they were removed, immigration to New York exploded. While many immigrants went to Chinatown, many others settled in Flushing, Queens (one of New York's five boroughs). Nowhere outside of Asia is home to more Chinese than New York.

Today, Flushing is the center of the New York Chinese food scene. Dumpling Galaxy, located in the Arcadia Mall (this is not unusual for Flushing Chinese restaurants), is raved about by locals and visitors alike.

Los Angeles

It may be surprising to learn that only New York has a larger Chinese population than Los Angeles. L.A. is therefore blessed with various forms of Chinese cuisine that all compete with each other, making it a popular destination to find great Chinese food. There are actually about 70,000 more Chinese people in Los Angeles than there are in San Francisco.

The development of the Los Angeles Chinatown began in 1871 when prospectors went south after failing to find fortune during California's Gold Rush. They established L.A.'s first Chinatown, which stood until the 1930s when it was demolished to build a train station. A new Chinatown emerged in 1938, a few blocks south of the old neighborhood, and it still thrives there today.

During the 1950s, when affordable transcontinental flights became available, Los Angeles' Chinatown was not only a destination for those living in Southern California but also became a popular spot for tourists to visit. It is now home to dozens of restaurants that serve authentic Chinese food, including Peking Duck, fresh seafood, and *dim sum*.

It is not Chinatown, however, that is most fondly discussed when the topic of great L.A. area Chinese food comes up. On that topic, experts and foodies set their sights to the east, all the way to the San Gabriel Valley. This area, just 15 miles from Chinatown, is the hotspot for Chinese cuisine in L.A. The Valley is home to close to two million people, about a quarter of which are Asian American, with Chinese being the largest group. Business people and professionals from

Diners eat dim sum *outdoors at a Chinese restaurant in Monterey Park, CA.*

Chapter 5 : Chinese Food in America   67

Taiwan spearheaded the Chinese influx when they began settling in the city of Monterey Park in the Valley during the 1970s, and it took off from there. Today, there are hundreds of Asian restaurants up and down Valley Boulevard. This includes popular Chinese spots such as Sea Harbour, located in Rosemead. Supporters swear it has the best dim sum in all of L.A.

American Chinese

The food in places like Flushing and the San Gabriel Valley is often hailed as being "authentic," meaning true to the way it would be prepared, cooked, and served in China. This is as opposed to the version of Chinese food now found in many Chinatown restaurants frequented by tourists and non-Chinese locals. This more mainstream food has been altered significantly to appeal to American tastes.

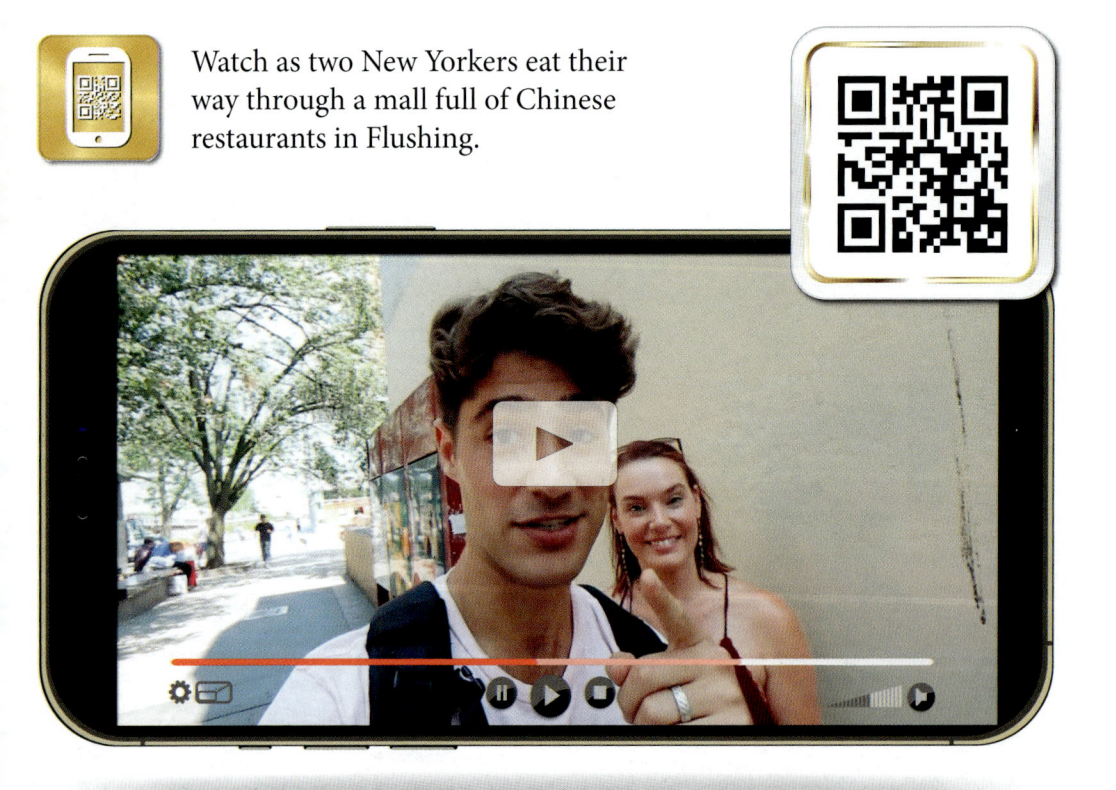

Watch as two New Yorkers eat their way through a mall full of Chinese restaurants in Flushing.

Chinese

Flushing, a city in Queens, NY is home to a large concentration of Chinese, who own dozens of businesses and restaurants in the area.

    Scholars believe that immigrants might not have started out with traditional dishes when they came to America. Those Chinese immigrants who came to California in the mid-1800s introduced Chinese food to America by opening their restaurants. These places served almost exclusively Cantonese-style cuisine, but the owners soon discovered that the American customers did not enjoy many authentic Chinese food flavors and textures. Over the next few decades, Chinese restaurant owners tinkered and experimented with their dishes, adding American ingredients and adjusting flavor profiles (think saltier). Eventually, smart owners developed two menus. The first was in Chinese and had dishes true in content and flavor to those their fellow Chinese customers remembered from

The American version of General Tso's chicken is battered and covered in a sweet, sticky sauce.

home. The second menu was in English and contained many newly invented "Chinese" dishes tailored to Americans. This American Chinese food spread across the country and was well established when those Chinese citizens who immigrated after 1965 arrived with fresh new examples of authentic Chinese cuisine.

Authentic Chinese food enclaves like Flushing and the San Gabriel Valley came to be because the business owners were catering to their own communities, not to tourists. They didn't need two menus, although the single menus have English on them now.

This Looks American

American Chinese cuisine has evolved over time. Thousands of Chinese restaurants exclusively serve American-style Chinese food. It has been Americanized in ways beyond flavor as well. There is fast food Chinese, mass-market Chinese, even table service franchise restaurant Chinese.

How do you tell the difference between American Chinese and the native cuisine? There are a few telltale signs.

Popular American Chinese dishes are sweet-and-sour chicken, beef broccoli stir fry, General Tso's chicken, pineapple shrimp fried rice, chop suey, and crab Rangoon. These dishes vary in how they are prepared and perhaps some minor ingredients that make up each dish, but they are remarkably consistent in any restaurant in the country, which is

TSO AMERICAN

Although General Tso's chicken is an American invention, the general himself was actually a real person. Tso was a 19th-century Hunanese soldier. Also, the dish itself does exist in China; it's a dish from the Hunan region. Other than the fact both use chicken, the American and Chinese versions have little in common. A Chinese American chef named Tsung Ting Wang was visiting Taiwan searching for inspiration before opening his restaurant in New York when he came across the dish. Wang liked the name but knew Americans wouldn't like the heavy, spicy, salty, and sour concoction. So, when he returned to New York, he invented his own dish (which is battered, deep-fried, and slathered in a sugary, sticky sauce) and put it on his menu with the now-famous name.

what Americans like. We are not looking for regional variations in our American Chinese food.

So, what makes these American? First of all, many are swimming in a thick, goopy sauce, which is not how the Chinese prepare their dishes. These are highly processed sauces that come out of a jug. Second, look at the ingredients. If you see broccoli (Chinese use

The chow mein sandwich is a popular item at fast food restaurants in the Northeast.

their native *gai lan* instead), tomatoes, pineapple, or carrots, that's another sign. These items are not used in Chinese cooking as they aren't native to the country. Then, of course, there's the dead giveaway…the fortune cookie, which is definitely not Chinese (they were invented in Japan).

Popular Staples

The American-style Chinese dish most commonly found at restaurants is either chop suey or chow mein. These dishes are certainly not as common as they used to be, however. The American term "chop suey" came from the Cantonese pronunciation of the phrase *tsap sui*, which in English means "odds and ends," which refers to the chopped pieces of meat found in the dish. "Chow Mein" is an American term based on the Chinese *chau men*, which means "fried noodles" and has its origins in Hong Kong, where Hakka chefs created it. It consists of stir-fried noodles mixed with bean sprouts, scallions, and soy sauce. The American versions use either flat (fried) or round (steamed) noodles. The steamed version is often mixed with onions, celery, carrots, and bean sprouts. The fried version is sometimes served as a sandwich.

Cantonese cuisine definitely has its purists, but just because it's American doesn't mean it can't be good. American Chinese food has become a style all its own. There are high-end Chinese restaurants across the country that serve American-style food and get top dollar for it. American-style restaurants have even opened across China, demonstrating that if done well, any kind of cuisine can be delicious.

Chinese food in America has evolved and changed over time to accommodate the American palate. With so many different regional styles of cuisine found throughout China, it's no surprise that we would find a variety of Chinese restaurants across our country today. From *dim sum* to General Tso's chicken, you don't need to travel halfway around the world for your favorite dish, traditional or American-style.

RESEARCH PROJECT

China has 23 other provinces that are not covered in this book. Choose one of them and do some research on its cuisine. Is it similar to that of one of the eight major regions, or does it have distinct characteristics of its own? Explain using details and specific examples. Then choose a dish from the region you selected and try to make it at home.

GLOSSARY OF KEY TERMS

Abalone: edible rock-clinging gastropod mollusks that have a flattened shell slightly spiral in form, lined with mother-of-pearl, and with a row of apertures along its outer edge

Affluent: having an abundance of goods or riches

Alluvial: related to or composed of clay, silt, sand, gravel, or similar detrital material deposited by running water

Bigoted: having or showing an attitude of hatred or intolerance toward the members of a particular group

Braising: to cook slowly in fat and a small amount of liquid in a closed pot

Dialect: a regional variety of language distinguished by features of vocabulary, grammar, and pronunciation from other regional varieties and constituting together with them a single language

Enclave: a distinct territorial, cultural, or social unit enclosed within or as if within foreign territory

Ethnic: of or relating to races or large groups of people who have the same customs, religion, origin, etc.

Feudal: a social system that existed in Europe during the Middle Ages in which people worked and fought for nobles who gave them protection and the use of land in return

Ginseng: a Chinese perennial herb having five leaflets on each leaf, scarlet berries, and an aromatic root used in herbal medicine especially in Eastern Asia

Glutinous: having the quality of glue

Hue: gradation of color

Influx: a coming in

Integral: of, relating to, or belonging as a part of the whole

Marinate: to steep food in a savory usually acidic sauce to enrich its flavor or to tenderize it

Monsoon: a periodic wind especially in the Indian Ocean and Southern Asia

Palate: the sense of taste

Peninsula: a portion of land nearly surrounded by water and connected with a larger body by an isthmus

Philosophy: a particular set of ideas about knowledge, truth, the nature and meaning of life, etc.

Processed: having been subjected to a special treatment (as in the course of manufacture)

Pungent: having an intense flavor or odor

Revelers: those who engage in noisy partying or merrymaking

Savory: having a spicy or salty quality without sweetness

Sorghum: a cereal grass having broad, corn-like leaves and a tall, pithy stem bearing the grain in a dense terminal cluster

Subtropical: pertaining to or occurring in a region between tropical and temperate

Typhoon: a hurricane occurring especially in the region of the Philippines or the China Sea

FURTHER READING & INTERNET RESOURCES

FURTHER READING

Banh, Jenny and Haiming Liu. *American Chinese Restaurants: Society, Culture and Consumption.* New York: Routledge, 2019.

Ch'ng, Poh Tiang. *100 Top Chinese Restaurants of the World.* Hong Kong: Prosperous Printing, 2020.

Qian, Suoqiao. *Chinese Culture: Its Humanity and Modernity.* Hackensack, NJ: World Scientific, 2021.

Yu, Ying-shih. *Chinese History and Culture: Sixth Century BCE to Seventeenth Century.* New York: Columbia University Press, 2016.

Zeng, Guojun, Henk J. de Vries, and Frank M. Go. *Restaurant Chains in China: The Dilemma of Standardisation versus Authenticity.* Singapore: Palgrave Macmillan, 2019.

INTERNET RESOURCES

https://www.livescience.com/28823-chinese-culture.html
Chinese Culture: Customs & Traditions of China

https://www.nationsonline.org/oneworld/Chinese_Customs/index.htm
Glossary of Chinese customs and traditions

https://ethnomed.org/resource/chinese-food-cultural-profile/
A cultural profile of Chinese food

https://www.seriouseats.com/introduction-hunan-chinese-cuisine
A Song of Spice and Fire: The Real Deal With Hunan Cuisine

https://www.thoughtco.com/history-of-chinese-opera-195127
A brief history of Chinese opera

INDEX

A
America, Chinese food in, 63–73
American Chinese, 68–70
Anhui Province, 21–30
    cuisine, 6, 27–29
    culture, 25–26
    Grand Canal, 21–22
    rural to modern, 24–25
    tale of one city, 22–23
    wild life, 29–30

B
Bagongshan dou fu (Bagongshan bean curd), 30
Bak chor mee (boiled dried noodles in sauce), 56
Bao cooking style, 15
Beijing, 13, 15
Bobo Kueh dish, 34–35
Boshan district of Zibo, 12
Braising, 43, 52
Buddha Jumps Over the Wall dish, 35

C
California Gold Rush, 33
Cantonese cuisine, 57–58, 73
Capsaicin, 41
Celebration. *See* Food/celebration/festivals
Chai tau kueh (savory cake stir-fried in soy sauce and garlic) dish, 56
Chaoshan region, 56
Char siu dish, 60, 61
Chengdu city, 37–38
Chili peppers, 39, 42
China, cuisine types in, 6. *See also* specific entries
Chinese Exclusion Act (1882), 65
Chizhou Nuo, 26
"Chop suey", 73
Chow-Fun snack, 64
"Chow Mein", 72, 73
Confucianism, 11
Cultural Revolution, 24
Culture
    Anhui Province, 25–26
    Fujian Province, 31–33
    Guangdong Province, 55–57
    Jiangsu and Zhejiang Provinces, 49–50
    Shandong Province, 11–14
    Sichuan and Hunan Provinces, 37–40

D
Daheyan pickle festival, in Jinan, 18
Dandan noodles, 17, 45
Deng Xiaoping, 49
Dezhou braised chicken dish, 18
Dim sum dishes, 61
Dong an zi ji (Dong'an chicken), 45
Douchi (fermented black beans), 42
Dragon Boat Festival, 43, 45
Dumpling Galaxy, 66

F
Flushing, 66, 69
Food/celebration/festivals
    in Anhui Province, 28
    in Chinese culture, 6
    in Fujian Province, 34–35
    in Guangdong Province, 59
    in Shandong Province, 17–19
    in Sichuan and Hunan Provinces, 44–45
    in Zhejiang and Jiangsu Provinces, 52–54
Fotiaoqiang dish, 35
Fujian Province, 30–35
    cuisine, 6, 33–34
    history and culture, 31–33
    traditional dishes, 34–35
Fuzhou city, 31, 34, 49

G
General Tso's chicken, 70, 71
Glass noodles, 42
Gold Rush, 63–64
Grand Canal, 21–22
Green chili peppers, 42
Guangdong Province, 54–61
    cooking styles and flavors, 57–58
    cuisine, 6
    dishes, 61
    food traditions and festivals, 59
    history and culture, 55–57
    trade fair, 56

H
Hakka cuisine, 34, 35
Han Chinese, 55
Han Dynasty, 47, 55
Hang Ah restaurant, 64
Hangzhou, 48
Heroin, 13
Ho, David, 64
Hong Shao Rou (braised pork belly), 45
Hongze Lake, 23
Hot pot (*Huo Guo*) food, 17, 44
Huizhou district, 30
Hunan Province. *See* Sichuan and Hunan Provinces
Hungry Ghosts Festival, 59
Huo Guo (hot pot food), 44

J
Jianbing dish, 18, 19
Jiangsu Province, 47
    celebration and food, 52–54
    cooking styles, 52
    cuisine, 6
    culture, 49–50
    history, 47–49
    seafood surplus, 50–51
Jiangxi cuisine, 40
Jianhuai/Jinhua. *See* Anhui Province

K
Kung Pao chicken, 45
Kunqu Opera, 49

L
La jiao dish, 40
Lantern Festival, 17

Chinese

Legalism, 11
Liu Bang, 47
Los Angeles, Chinese food in, 66–68
Lower Yangtze. *See* Jiangsu Province
Luzhou roast duck, 30

M
Málà (*numbing spice*), 41, 42
Manchu people, 49
Manchurian language, 49
Mandarin language, 49
Mao Zedong, 24, 39, 49
Mapo Tofu dish, 17, 45
Mid-Autumn Festival, 52, 53
Minnan language, 49
Moon Festival, 34, 53
Mooncakes, 53–54
Mount Tai, 10, 11

N
New York, Chinese food in, 64–66
Numbing spice (*málà*), 41, 42
Nuo Opera, 25–26

O
Opiate, 13
Opium Wars, 12, 13, 33

P
Pearl River Delta, 55
Peng kway dish, 59
"People's communes", 39
Pichai Yuan (Qingdao), 14
Pingshu (storytelling art), 50
Pixian Douban sauce, 42
Polo, Marco, 31
Pork meat, 16

Q
Qin Dynasty, 47, 55
Qingming Festival (Tomb Sweeping Festival), 18, 28–29, 34
Qingming Kueh dish, 34–35
Qu Yuan, 45

R
Red chili peppers, 42
Rice noodles, 58

S
Sam Wo Restaurant, 64
San Francisco, Chinese food in, 63–64
Seafood, in Shandong cuisine, 16
Shandong Province, 9–19
    ancient culture, 11–14
    celebrations and food, 17–19
    ingredients of dishes, 16–17
    primary goal, in cooking, 15, 16
    Yellow River, 9
    cuisine, 6, 15, 16
    Mount Tai, 10, 11
    Opium Wars, 12, 13
Shefan dinner, 39

Shenzhen city, 54
Shuma dish, 61
Sichuan and Hunan Provinces, 37–45
    celebrating with food, 44–45
    cooking techniques, 43
    cuisines, 6, 41–43
    history and culture, 37–40
Sizhou city, 22–23
Smoking (cooking technique), 43, 52
Song Sao dish, 54
Soy sauce, 58
Spring Festival (Chinese New Year), 18, 44
Standard Mandarin language, 49
Steamed Noodles with Pork Ribs, 57
Steaming (cooking style), 43, 52, 57
Stewed Chicken with Three Cups of Sauce, 40
Stewing, 52
Stir-fry techniques, 43, 52
Sui Dynasty, 56
Sweet and sour carp dish, 18

T
Taiping Rebellion, 32–33
Taishan. *See* Mount Tai
Tang Dynasty, 15
Tang Yuan dish, 19
Tea production, 52
Tomb Sweeping Festival, 18
Trade fair, in Guangzhou, 56

W
Wang, Tsung Ting, 71
Water Splashing Festival, 27
West Lake Vinegar Fish, 54
White pepper, 58
Wok cooking pot, 57–58
Wuyi Mountains, 30, 31

X
Xiaochi (small eats), 51
Xie ke huang (crab shell yellow), 30

Y
Yangtzee River, 24
Yangzhou fried rice, 54
Yellow River, 9, 23

Z
Zha Jiang Mian dish, 15, 17
Zhaliang dish, 61
Zhejiang Province, 47
    celebration and food, 52–54
    cooking styles, 52
    cuisine, 6
    culture, 49–50
    history, 47–49
    seafood surplus, 50–51
    tea production, 52
Zhejiang University, in Hangzhou, 52
Zhou Dynasty, 11
Zhu Yuanzhang, 53
Zongzi food, 45

Index 79

AUTHOR'S BIOGRAPHY

PETER DOUGLAS is a former journalist, reporting on both general news and sports for many years at local TV affiliates in the Midwest. He has traveled across Europe and Asia, experiencing and enjoying the food in every port of call. When he's not writing, Peter enjoys traveling and spending time with his wife and two children. If he's not watching lacrosse or a choral performance, you're likely to find him at a hockey game.

CREDITS

SHUTTERSTOCK:
Pg 1: New Africa, 2 & 74: MaraZe, 2: kongsky, 7: Andrew Krasovitckii, 8: asharkyu, xiaorui, Phairoh chimmi, kram-9, gkrphoto, Amam ka 10: Hanyu Qiu, 11: StrippedPixel.com, 14: Kapi Ng, 16: norikko, 17: atiger, 19: Alessio Ferreri, 20: Africa Studio, SOMMAI, kazu326, Ivanna Pavliuk, Piotr Krzeslak, Khumthong, Riccio da favola, 22: rodho, 23: He jinghua, 24: chuyuss, 25: Adao Studiio, 27: yeangxi, 28: Mark Brandon, 29: Nungning20, 31: wzlv, 32: Everett Collection, 35: thefoodgrapher, 36: Photoongraphy, Pixel-Shot, pilipphoto, Dipak Shelare, Paul Pellegrino, kasarung, Jula Store 38: B.Zhou, 39: SteAck, 40: HiTecherZ, 42: Virginia Garcia, 44: Alamin Chowdhury, 46: JIANG HONGYAN, Larisa Blinova, My Kids, Alena_Kos, pilipphoto, nadianb, Dipak Shelare, 48: Govanz, 49: Hung Chung Chih, 50: cherry-hai, 51: Q'ju Creative, 53: gu min, 54: Eric007, 56: Nadir Keklik, 58: Amarita, 60: Alexander Prokopenko, 61: bonchan, 62: DronG, 65: travelview, 67: Ringo Chiu, 69: James Andrews1, 70: sockagphoto, 74: Kzenon

WIKIMEDIA COMMONS:
12: Edward Duncan, 57: N509FZ, 72: Rikomatic

Chinese